Inspirations *of a* Sensitive Heart

BELENDA STEPHEN CYPRESS

WESTBOW
PRESS®
A DIVISION OF THOMAS NELSON
& ZONDERVAN

WestBow Press books may be ordered through booksellers or by contacting:

WestBow Press
A Division of Thomas Nelson & Zondervan
1663 Liberty Drive
Bloomington, IN 47403
www.westbowpress.com
1 (866) 928-1240

ISBN: 978-1-5127-2903-0 (sc)
ISBN: 978-1-5127-2904-7 (hc)
ISBN: 978-1-5127-2902-3 (e)

Library of Congress Control Number: 2016901619

Print information available on the last page.

WestBow Press rev. date: 2/19/2016

Contents

A Good Morning

As a brand-new day began for me,
I wondered what choices to make,
For I felt a special calming
Once my mind lay there awake.

I have no questions anymore,
And it doesn't matter why.
I feel this peace has covered me.
I cannot help but cry

A happy sob when no one else
Could reward me with this thrill—
It's a gift of true compassion
From whatever my God has willed.

Even once I start to think of things
I pray will turn out right,
For now, at least, I'm pleased,
I was kept throughout last night.

September 23, 2015

One Year Anniversary

I'm trying to think what day it was.
How did I come to feel?
Jerry opened his gentle heart to me
With his expression of love so real.

I wonder—did I respond to him
With a proper, appropriate word,
At least to give him something back
With what he so deserved?

I was pleasantly kind of nervous.
I was young, and I was shy,
Usually felt light-headed
Just before I would start to cry.

What I see right now is clear
As I knew also back then.
How sweet to celebrate a together life
Rather than what day that may have been,

For the forty-four years I spent with him
Were filled with deep delight.
This quality man was special—
He made my life just right.

I realize I've been so, so blessed
Now I've missed him for one year.
I'm ever so grateful for becoming one,
For I'll always feel him near.

June 10, 2015

Another Chance

May God create a mind-set
In which I see him more,
Awaken my sense of awesomeness
That I never quite knew before,

For I'm poised to venture onward
On paths I have not known.
I'm sure of it, bless God above,
'Cause He's watched me as I've grown.

I don't have it down just right,
And with every deed I chose,
Even with a magic ball,
It's impossible to get real close.

Reverencing him precisely,
Thinking, *What things I've missed,*
What joy in spirit I could have had
Just remembering he still exists.

If I could have a do-over
So my life would be less worn,
If I could dictate what and when
From the moment I was born,

I'd more than likely do much worse
And forget to laugh and dance.
Please, God, don't let me falter long.
Do give me one more chance.

July 8, 2015

Apology

How can you show me love so much
And refuse to turn away,
Especially when I'm lashing out
And not careful what I say?

How is it that I fail to see
How serious you are and bold,
You're not begrudging anything
But I'm different ... I feel cold.

The more-than-frequent days and months
When it's hard for me to cope,
I feel like I can scream inside
And I'm ready to give up hope.

It must be me and what I am
Does logic have to cease?
If I don't start to change myself
How can I talk of peace?

Do I warrant a little empathy
For what I thought I said?
Didn't mean for things to unravel
Before I go to bed?

I want to be convinced again
That it's just a matter of time
A calmness that I see in you
Can possibly too be mine.

I don't want to feel today,
That all I do is cry.
Or continually need to probe myself
And always ask me—why?

If God should allow me peace inside
And the ability to express,
I pray he'll richly amaze you
You certainly deserve his best.

December 26, 1990

Appreciating You, Pastor

Time after time I've heard you speak,
And it wasn't very hard
To see revelations brought out
That all our lives are marred.

I perceive more minds will slowly shift
Including this fragile one
When God's anointing comes through strong
As you help his will be done.

To bring the Word unblemished
And remind us God is near,
Pastor, you are much appreciated,
For making it all so clear.

I'm hoping exceptional rewards will come
From years of study and sweat,
You bring such powerful messages.
Showing God's not finished here yet.

July 20, 2015

Assurance

For reasons, I am trying to say,
Few persons impress me so.
I cannot tell you why this is,
Because I just don't know.

Why some just have a lack of care
And go about their way,
Not displaying too much common
sense;
To what wise men have to say.

I assure you, if you're doubtful,
There's no one else for me;
You enhanced my world and all my
life,
So forever this love shall be.

Many things I know by instinct now,
Can't help but shine inside,
Sort of like a sunshine
That glows from inner pride.

Yep, I'm filled with happiness.
Do you notice that it is true?
You should really see with ease
I beam because of you.

I try to convey a special way
How I've grown to love you, dear.
I hope your spirit can comprehend
How much I am sincere.

Making sure we do not cave
To any silly strife,
I reassure you once again
I'm so proud to be your wife.

March 19, 1971

Birthday Time

Birthday time is special,
So here's a little thought,
And here's a little gift of love
I liked for you and bought.

The price is not important so much;
It's a blessing from the Lord.
A simple wish for a special day
With a gift I can afford.

Mothers are specially made each day.
They come in different sizes.
They're varied in many other ways,
And ages are sure surprises.

Age alone is nothing more
Than numbers that come and go.
Numbers don't tell the story of
The deeds of good they sow.

Just a name doesn't represent
How mothers toiled and cried
To give their best in all of life
As a strong and able guide.

But as I grow in age each day,
I learn what things I see.
In you is such a mother
I will never, ever be.

Happy birthday and love always.

April 24, 1974

Caregivers' Poem

As I study and prepare for classes here,
And I take an active part,
I'm reminded God should rule
My helping hands and heart.

When I invite God's Holy Spirit,
I love more of his Son.
It's a privilege to be a part of grace,
Like I'm the only one.

'Cause when I recall Christ's mercy
For people just like us,
How can we not but give him
A committed heart to trust?

What a joy indeed to have this chance,
Knowing fragile life will end,
To gather with and acquaint ourselves
And call each other friend.

Let's rejoice and focus on giving care
By remembering the day he rose,
For we will not be finished here
Even when our books are closed.

January 7, 2015

Casting My Care on You

If it seems like I have doubts about
What direction I should go,
It's because I'm not yet confident,
But I'm positive God will know.

Right now I'm in a job I do
That shatters my peace and rest.
Did destiny lead me to this place
To develop me for my best?

I do believe the written truth,
God says to cast my care.
I'm compelled to stand, though I'm afraid,
Even when it's hard to bear!

God has to have a word for me—
He's still my closest friend.
I seek him to just fix this thing
And make this quandary end.

Please keep my faith from wavering
When things get really tough.
I stand on what you anointed, Lord,
For your grace is quite enough.

July 13, 2015

Cherishing a Child

With love for my daughters, Noella, Stephanie, and Samantha

I wonder if every daddy's aware
How significant is his child,
And does he develop that special gift
While he spoils them for a while?

I'm curious if they're *not* newborns,
Does he keep a smiling eye?
If ever the child might show off some,
Why must he make them cry?

And how should they remember Dad?
Will it be what things he'll say?
Then assure them there is *nothing*
That can take his love away.

Children sometimes get weepy too,
But I understand their tears.
They need their daddy's approval
To cherish them through their years.

I know that my three daughters
Thought Dad could do no wrong.
For sure, the legacy he left behind
Is making them wise and strong.

September 15, 2015

Choir

The choir sang the hymns of old,
And applause filled the air.
They sang of God's amazing grace
And of his love and care.

Little they knew I had that dream
Just the other night,
And Christ assured my heavy heart
That things would be all right.

So the voices of the choir meant more
Than merely words and rhyme.
They showed the Lord was blessing me
And had been all the time.

They also said no matter how
I chose to live this life,
If first I put the Lord in all,
He'd be my help and guide.

October 31, 1972

Christian Duty

Sometimes we fail to realize
Just whom we need to please.
Sometimes we assume it's useless
Spending time on bended knees.

Sometimes we go as far to say
We shall work it out just fine.
We don't need devotion
To give the Lord much time.

It matters not how young we are;
The goal is still the same.
The Lord's work is serious
And never has been a game.

The body of the entire church
Is one of different parts;
Each hand has a job to do
But through sincerest hearts.

Combining the talents of many
To lift the name of Christ
Enables the young and aged alike
To get more out of life.

We must depend on God for strength
To do what he has willed.
Through faith He'll lift our heavy
load
To climb our personal hill.

So our duty is to work to build
An example for those who follow.
If we live and commit for Christ's
sake,
There will be great things tomorrow.

November 13, 1972

Christmas and You

I wish I were a poet to let
You know the things I feel,
The love I have within me—
I want to show it's real.

It's more than hugs and kisses
When things are going rotten.
It's even more than love pats
When the aches are long forgotten.

It is something you can try to say,
But then halfway through
You find that you are stuck for words,
So you mumble, "I love you."

It's sometimes when my eyes meet yours
And then I look away
Not because I'm being rude,
(Don't know quite how to say).

Except you have a certain way
That never fails to ease
My troubling mind—yes, dear,
Your affection is what I need.

You might think this Christmas card
Is meant to be a gag.
It really isn't—just letting you know
The thoughts of you I had.

A personal touch from me to you
For now and years to come
To say I tenderly love you
In many more ways than one.

December 17, 1970

Church

There may not be a better time
To glance through the year,
To contemplate the good and bad,
How God has been so near.

It seems a good idea for me
To glance back through the past,
To learn from our mistakes
And appreciate all we've had.

Some may be sad and ask
How we can go ahead,
But God's comfort surrounds us.
Indeed, that's what he said.

Think on things that lift us
And of others not as brave;
Share the still-good news
To those that are not saved.

Remember there's beauty around us.
Just open our eyes and see;
The blessings we have each minute
Don't really have to be.

We have to play a part in life
And choose the time to pause,
Put forth our earnest efforts
To further the greater cause.

Let's firmly resolve right now
To start a simple list,
To treat others as we want ourselves
Without much selfishness.

The Church is us … and if we know
That victory exists,
We can submit ourselves to right,
And the devil we can resist.

For we don't boast perfection—
We wrestle in our sin—
But without a doubt, be confident,
We're conquerors in the end.

Here's a message for all of us:
We have much work to do,
But the reward is so tremendous
When this fight is finally through.

We cannot wait another day.
Plenty of time has passed,
Church that exists inside our souls
Will set us free at last.

April 11, 1972

Contented

Miscommunication creeps up,
And lately I've gotten a hint
That it's not always what we say
But what, in fact, was meant.

The more one tries to explain it out
From a selfish point of view,
The more it makes things messier.
Though you're aware what's right to do.

Taking time to approach and talk
With conversation short or long,
Some people really think they're right
But are sincerely wrong.

And things like that will happen
As long as people live.
I'm mindful to practice one fervent word,
That word is just *forgive.*

September 23, 2015

Daddy's Big Baby

If you've never had a chance, my friends,
To shake his gentle hand,
A kind and caring heart of gold—
Well, this was such a man.

> I saw him as a gentle giant,
> He stood so strong and tall.
> I always felt so safe with him,
> Was not afraid at all.

> > Maybe by being his baby girl
> > I sometimes got my way,
> > But I believe he did not mind
> > (I'd really have to say).

> > > I used to like my ice cream!
> > > Around four years old or more,
> > > And if I managed to smile at him,
> > > He'd hurry out to the store.

> > > > He taught me by his character
> > > > What's important to keep in mind,
> > > > How to have a peaceful heart
> > > > By practicing being kind.

> > > > > He left us with a word today.
> > > > > The message is quite clear:
> > > > > On purpose, we should express true love
> > > > > Every day that we are here.

> > > > > > I won't forget how blessed I am,
> > > > > > 'Cause I'll remember at least I had
> > > > > > A God-fearing man to model my life.
> > > > > > I'm so proud to call him Dad.

October 25, 2014

Dear Heart

I imagine at that blessed place
Where his birth had been foretold,
The sacredness of the Christ child
Was a gift for Mary to hold.
She must have looked at tiny eyes
And held his little hand,
Caressed that little baby face
As only a mother can.
She must have been so overwhelmed
To see that promise real,
Knowing she actually had given birth –
What a love she had to feel.
She probably wanted to stay awake
Feeling breath one after another,
While thanking God so passionately
For selecting her as his mother.

December 17, 2015

Dear Mama

Mama, there is no one else
In my life I care for more;
Maybe that's the reason
I want my love to pour.

Pour out what you're deserving
That I may help at least
To make a difference in your life
And days for you are sweet.

If only I could turn time back
To when I was a girl
And things were so, so simple
Throughout my little world.

I'd find more time to laugh and sing
And take an active part
In things you'd like to do yourself
Just from the very start.

Everything that comes my way,
What issues I might see;
I have the belief, no matter what,
You're always there for me.

I wouldn't be so busy
Either away or here at home
That I couldn't find ten minutes
To visit you or to phone.

In other words, I'll do better
I haven't done all I can;
I didn't neglect on purpose—
That *was not* in the plan.

But I promise you in the future,
I will show you I'm sincere;
I will say nice things more often
So you'll see that I'm still near.

Love You.

November 19, 1990

Dear Mom

You've made so many things go right
That popped up from nowhere;
You've showed me time and time again
How very much you care.

You've done so many things for me
As you already know;
I thought I'd write in my own words,
Dear Mom, I love you so.

I must admit there were plenty of times
I failed to act the part;
I failed to show just what I felt
And what was in my heart.

I let go by opportunities
To appreciate what you do;
I just don't know where I would be
Without dear Mother—you!

I know I owe you so much more;
I really don't have a lot,
But I hope you like this little gift
And understand its thought.

For money can't buy the precious ways
You've stuck by each of us;
The times we started acting smart,
You had a right to fuss.

But now this is a special time.
Happy birthday on today.
Your daughters truly love you, Mom,
Lots more than we can say.

April 21, 1971

Depressed

I've read and heard of people
Who come to lose their mind.
Does this happen rather quickly
Or over a span of time?

Thinking that I'm chivalrous
And a sensitive, caring being,
You'd think I'd be more fortified
And understand life's meaning.

I feel so lost and empty,
For no one seems sincere;
I need to *know* to what degree
You desire my presence near.

I'm tired of being emotional
I brood or cry lots more,
Find out why and listen, please—
Oh, my heart gets mighty sore.

It's not entirely anatomy
Or problems we solve in bed;
Sometimes I can be satisfied
By beautiful words you've said.

My life is wrapped up tightly.
I so depend on you
For where I need to venture out
And the routine things I do—

Maybe a snack or little something
When we plan a date as one,
Include a talk about work
That I'm trying to overcome.

We don't include any others
As entertainment in our life,
I'd like to think you're not afraid
To share some of your wife.

Well, we can enjoy a private dance,
Something simple such as this.
Prance around the living room
To capture what laughter missed.

Trying to avoid a boring life,
Expecting to celebrate more,
We'll both find life fulfilling
Once we unlock that exciting door.

January 3, 1992

20

Do You Know Why It's So Hard?

When I saw your cranky moods,
I'd quickly give you drink
Or soothe your brow with lullabies
For mellow thoughts to think.

I'd clasp your little face in hands
What deep and pretty eyes.
You'd peer up with such sweetness;
I prayed you'd grow up wise.

I wrote a poem and smiled
'Cause you weighed upon my heart.
The need to give you special love
I attempted to well impart;

I somehow knew it would come
one day—
It was traumatic nonetheless.
I prayed to teach you right from
wrong;
I really tried my best.

I had you when I was quite young,
I was green myself, you know—
A lot of times I was unsure
Which way I was to go.

Though I may not have known too
much,
I prayed a constant plea
That if the Lord would watch my
child,
I'd serve him thankfully.

The child is grown to womanhood
From days and months to years.
Lullabies have hushed up now
And I don't dry your tears.

But when I see you struggle
Over things that should not be,
I have to force myself to wait
Till help is asked of me.

Because I understand much more
Than what you think I do,
I know some things that cause you
pain
Because I mothered you.

I have no intention to insist
That you heed my beck and call;
It just makes it good all round
For communication shared for all.

I want for you the best
As I did so in the past.
It's hard to wonder how long
Your concerns have to last.

I'm committed to be available.
My aim is to be wise.
You only need to come to me
Understand I'm on your side.

January 20, 2012

Don't You Worry

I was quite dismayed today—
What happened lit a fuse;
Already the day was sort of weird
Before I got the news.

You mustn't forget at times like this,
Through things you really dread;
All you do is keep the faith
And firmly forge ahead.

If you can praise in trouble's midst,
And see what's going on;
We pretty much can recognize
It's time that we grow strong,

Try to remember who stands in charge
In spite of all the knocks;
It can help to reassure us
That Christ is still the Rock.

He'll see, for sure, our needs are met,
That's what the scriptures told.
He not a man that he should lie
Or leave us in the cold.

If nothing was allowed to happen
To test how we go through,
We wouldn't have the strength
To do all we could do.

We'd almost leave this world the same
As we came to exist,
Think of all the abundance
We would have sorely missed.

Though you and I are different
I empathize how you feel,
I just know God's got your back;
And be sure he always will.

August 26, 1991

Each and Every

Often I like to try to
Write about my thoughts;
I like to write down things
What joys to me you've brought.

I like to try to make you see
That on my truth and honor,
I'm glad I'm part of life with you
As I keep on growing stronger.

There seems to be a special way
That can be seen in you;
It comes to surface all the time
With everything you do.

Funny, but I just can't seem
To give this thing a name;
All I know it's sort of like
A wispy little pain

That soothes the heart when
Everything goes sour.
I cherish this wonderful love—
This binding love of ours.

It's kind of hard to write
Exactly what I wish,
So would you like to settle for
A smile, a hug, a kiss?

I hope one day it's clear
What I'm really trying to say;
I will cherish the time you gave to me
Each minute, each hour, each day.

February 24, 1971

Enjoy the Day

When you got through your daily rounds,
Did you accomplish one small task?
Did you matter once to someone else?
Are you comfortable if I ask?

Did you at least attempt to show
Your talent to soothe and lift?
Were you challenged to remember that
You shared your special gift?

Did you notice someone cried today?
Did you carry some extra weight?
Did you take on more decisions
That others were to make?

What did you learn from living
A day that started new?
Did *you* improve and do your best
The same you always do?

I hope both eyes weren't focused down
And the noise didn't sound too loud
So you could marvel at that rising sun
And the parting of the cloud.

I trust you did not miss out
On things that make you glad.
Capture more the simple things
You weren't conscience that you had.

July 15, 2015

Family and Friends

Once in a while it's good to take
The time to think within,
To meditate on what we call
A dear and special friend.

Well, it's one who shows
encouragement
No matter if he's way 'cross town;
He'll gladly lend a friendly ear
When others let you down.

He always wants the best for you,
And rightfully he should;
If you're blessed with bigger bucks,
That too is well and good.

He'll tell you what you
ought to know
And just where you ought to be;
And both your desires for victory
Should include the family.

Really, you *all* are family,
So I guess we all are kin;
Some are tall and some are short,
And a few are not so thin.

You know, we sometimes
start out wrong,
Set out on a different quest,
But remember the Lord took care
And loves us nonetheless.

Happiness for me is loving
As humbly as a lamb
With strength, poise,
and confidence
In *who* and where I am.

Being a blessing to those we touch,
Feeling great to do our best
To stand against the hardships
And try to pass life's test.

Glory to God for his mercy!
We've another chance to say
We love each friend and family.
We're *all* so blessed today.

I can look back now on yesterdays
To perceive how this might end;
I'm delighted to say it's beautiful.
You're a family and a friend.

July 26, 1991

Filling in Time

Another lazy day at work
When time all but stands still;
We've eaten tons of food and drink—
Oh boy, we had our fill!

We've stretched our bodies far and wide
And went outside to sun,
Looked at watches umpteen times,
And yawned and yawned and yawned.

I can choose to hang around
Or politely take a seat,
But any work I got right now
Would really be a treat.

My nails were polished meticulously;
I neatly groomed my hair.
I read those lousy directives—
As if somebody cares.

Oh, well. They say to enjoy myself;
This too is going to pass.
Good thing—I can't imagine
My sanity much longer can last.

July 29, 1992

Finding Focus

Bear with me for a little while,
My thoughts right now are slow
Was that the answer I searched for?
Well, in time I'll surely know.

Because it's still quite possible
I'll share ... I'll laugh ... I'll smile—
Don't really know with whom or where,
So it just might take a while.

Assuredly, time will have a way
Of showing just who is real.
Ulterior motives will show themselves
In spite of how we feel.

In the meantime, I must concentrate,
Be brave, and not to whine,
Learn the will of God for me
And where I am assigned.

I'll try to recognize happiness
In whatever state I'm in,
Compelled to keep inspiring thoughts,
And try to be a friend.

I'll pray for more serenity
As I'm granted all my needs,
Listen and submit to wisdom,
And hope that he is pleased.

September 9, 2015

Forgive Me ...

Sometimes it might not seem as though
I mean the things I say;
Sometimes it might be hard for you
To brighten up my day.

Sometimes I might get stubborn and
Refuse to show a smile;
In other words, sometimes I might
Have ways just like a child.

These only represent the things
I'm figuring out myself;
I'm disappointed for the things *I* did
And not with someone else.

Because that thought has come to me,
Accept instead this truth:
Those things I did are really not
The things I feel toward you.

So, darling heart, forgive me
for those moments of despair;
Remind me that you meant it when
You said you really care.

My wonderful one, as always,
If you just only knew,
As you give your love to me,
I'll give my love to you.

Let's pledge to keep this marriage
Truly a blessing from above,
That from this day forevermore,
We'll share each other's love.

January 26, 1971

Forgiving

Do you remember when not long ago
We didn't have a dime?
We had little food and extras
But were careful not to whine.

We found it not too hard
To smile and laugh and sing,
Because we hoped for better things
That tomorrow would surely bring.

Well, the days indeed got better,
And we're finally over the hump;
We even bought a house and car
(And became rather pleasantly
plump).

Together we made an effort
To worship with people who try
To seek the Lord just like we did
For one day all will die.

The life we had was good indeed,
With more blessings to divide;
We appreciated all the little things
And never were filled with pride.

If we saw one touched by struggles
And we had a hand to lend,
We didn't mind to try and be
A quick and ready friend.

Yes, we possessed material things
That we could simply store
More than that all blessings
Made us grateful that much more.

And because we so are mindful,
We were blessed to be so—
Didn't need to question reasons,
Didn't really need to know.

We saw a God who cares for us,
Who provided a bountiful feast;
We acknowledge he sustains our life
And offers abundant peace.

But we can't have that perfect peace
If we're stubborn and poised to fight,
If we get upset over nothing
And think we're always right.

I've been through sickness, somewhat;
I've experienced hunger pain.
But I've also been in awe
Again, and again, and again.

Sometimes there've been some
accidents
Where I could walk away,
And I cried with a thankful heart
I was spared another day,

Confined in a local hospital
Where a stranger became a friend,
Not knowing for sure if ever again
I'd see a day's end.

Danger unseen was shielded,
And I hurt no one by wreck.
There've been a few close calls,
Thank God, I kept my neck.

Life's been good, in other words,
So how can I forget?
Why is it still so easy
To complain and fuss or fret?

I tell myself to rejoice and praise,
'Cause I don't want to be
One to waste these priceless gifts
That were purposely given me.

Let's not have fear to open up;
We know we all have sinned
Trying to make it upward means
Sometimes our minds must bend.

People out there are suffering
And would give their very arm
To enjoy what things I have,
So I don't see the harm

In trying to think on *good* things
And give each other a break;
Look instead at my own faults
And also at my mistakes.

I don't always know the pains
That I should keep or share,
And I don't always know just why
I just don't leave it there.

At least it's clear and easier
To figure how to succeed:
First be ready to forgive and love
And provide each other's need.

It's possible to get kinda selfish
And do some stupid stuff;
Whether or not we admit it,
We close our eyes to such.

At times even ears are closed—
We learned that from a youth—
But it's high time to let it go
And face the honest truth.

As long as God has woken me up
To see another day,
I petition that I'm forgiven—
More grace, oh Lord, I pray.

December 4, 1991

Frustration

I know frustration is amplified
If I'm having not good a day
Or even if the moon is full,
So what am I trying to say?

I'm saying it had to start somewhere.
Some *thing* was sure the cause;
I didn't imagine this disaster
Upon me would fall.

What I did was just forget
That whenever I look to find
Someone to quickly please me,
I am delusional or I am lying,

Because I learned quite long ago
There is no other Joe or Jim
To totally fill this void
Or to cater to my whim.

I wish my mouth couldn't form itself
To utter what I feel;
Might that cure what's ailing me
Like medicine when I'm ill?

Will you gently try to assure me
With a strong, compassionate word,
That it's only temporary
Even when I sound absurd.

It doesn't really work as well
Without quality time, I'm told,
And sensing a bit half-heartedness
It's futile to crave control.

Eventually it should dawn on me:
Hey, wait a minute there;
I'm getting depressed for wanting.
Is that really being fair?

My frustration is only temporary—
So very glad that's true—
And the quickest way to dispel it
Is to take a breath or two.

I'm ready to take a breath
And not conclude so fast;
One thing I am now confident—
Surely, this will eventually pass.

December 13, 1991

God Bless America

"God bless America, all of us,"
Is our continual prayer.
We all are part of what goes on,
And so we all should care.

The war is almost over, and
Our gleeful hearts will roam;
Oh what a joy to have our boys
Finally all back home.

As Americans, we should honor
God first,
And we give him praise deserved;
Our conscience esteems to honor
our flag,
And so we proudly serve.

Men and women whose families
remain
Keep the vigil bright;
They listened for any bits of news
That their loved ones were all right.

They can rejoice for any good message
That fighting may have ceased,
And maybe just a little while
The world can know some peace.

But you know what really happened?
Just why the war was brief?
Why things transpired the way
they did
To give our lives relief?

The prayers of the righteous saints
Are what the Master heard.
It was his mercy and grace and
might
To only say the word.

He looked beyond our sinfulness,
And with his loving hand,
He made a way that we could start
To restore the shattered land.

How great the Lord we serve today!
We need to live more right
And show others how they can love
Instead of how to fight.

February 28, 1991

God Is Love

L   is for the life he gave
      So you and I might see;

O   means He's the only way
      By which we can be free.

V   is for the voice that speaks
      When his word reveals his will;

E   is everlasting life
      When with him we'll one day live.

Redeemed through everything he had
No other way we can
Please him but to show love, too,
To each our fellow man.

December 30, 1971

Good Lord

My Lord has always loved me
His grace is warm and kind.
I now have seen that I am his,
And Jesus is personally mine.

To feel his closeness wrap around
My spirit and my soul—
It makes me never be concerned
Of slowly growing old.

When each and every time I'm touched,
I feel it's oh so new!
I sense that air of love breeze by,
I stand firm 'til it's through.

How can I help but praise my Lord?
I will never *not* believe
His attention and love, so evident
And he has made me pleased.

My Father, I pray to grow in strength,
To put you first in all,
To share the things I want to have,
To heed your beck and call.

For no one else sustains me;
I definitely have a friend.
I heard and believe your promise
That you'll be here till the end.

December 29, 1971

Good Luck

Let me be outlandish
And say life's just a test;
You didn't ask and sure didn't want
To go through all this mess.

If you think things should be perfect,
You're living a great big lie;
We all will have some issues
Until the day we die.

I know you may be thinking,
There *are* times when it may seem
The only way you're making it
Is through a peaceful dream.

And then you start remembering
That sometimes dreams come true,
So hold on to your hope, my friend,
And do what you should do.

I may not have experience
In what is on your plate,
But I want to encourage you with this poem
And hope I'm not too late.

Hang in there …

March 14, 1971

Good Night

Now I lay my head to rest.
I've done the best I know.
Time to wave so long to things
That crowd my sense with woe.

I really don't need to summarize.
Not as bad as it might seem.
I tell myself to just calm down—
I'm tired tonight … just dream.

Tomorrow will be another day.
Bless God; it'll be all right.
I'm sure He's got me covered well
On whatever ground I fight.

For the battles are meant to remind me
Even when I'm thinking wrong
I must not doubt my most high God.
He's the one who keeps me strong.

Blessings …

July 10, 2015

Good-bye

You guys somewhat know me
And know I like to write,
So I wanted to share a thought or two
Before I took to flight.

One notable thing I've learned quite well—
Life's dilemmas drip like rain,
But they make us more appreciative
For all our little gains.

Our faces and names are different,
We've varied degrees of fame,
But in the end it's obvious
Our desires are all the same.

A hearty laugh has done us good,
Hanging out with regular folk,
A smile at something charming,
Or a halfway funny joke.

Working with y'all will be treasured.
Yes, I do believe I'm set;
I'll applaud all that has happened
And have not one regret.

Whatever managed to bring us here
To excel in what we do,
We're now a part of history
We were meant to travel through.

The job hasn't always gone as planned.
Some days were very long,
But I certainly did a bang-up job
So this change for me ain't wrong.

July 27, 1992

Gracious

These bones may one day weaken,
And these eyes and legs may go;
Friends might even vanish,
But this one thing I know:

A virgin bore a perfect child,
And he grew to be a man,
Went about his Father's work
All up and down the land.

For thirty-three years he obeyed him;
He healed the blind and lame.
He can visit us in his spirit;
Christ Jesus is his name.

Oh how precious it feels to meet him,
To finally get to see
And have him mold and shape us
Into whatever we need to be.

Let's graciously honor and glorify
Our Father up above
And pray He'll graciously touch us
With an abundance of his love.

April 20, 1984

Grow with Me

Today is not a holiday;
It has no special name.
I just felt like telling you
I love you just the same.

Every now and then, you see,
I have to make it clear
I love you just as much right now
As I would if you were here.

Though I admit it would be great
To have you close at hand,
To think of a way to convince you
So you can smile and understand.

You don't holler when I'm wrong
And stress out with my temper
And never got the rolling pin
If I dared to burn your supper.

Knowing things have gotten confused,
Well, a couple times or two,
There's still no problem in making it
As we travel this journey through.

So I am in a frame of mind
As we enjoy the age of youth.
The exceptional things describing you
Are nothing but the truth.

Grow with me and lend your heart
For just a life-time longer;
This powerful love between us two
Can't help but make us stronger.

March 16, 1971

Had I Looked Ahead

What if I had previewed this life
As I cradled inside the womb?
Suppose I could've chose myself,
What traits would I assume?

I would have glimpsed many
glorious days
The ones I wanted to see,
But what about those darkened days,
That turn to tragedy?

And what if I'd been able
To manipulate things ahead.
Would I become high-minded
As I stoutly bragged and said …

I can simply convince myself,
I'll do all right all right,
Believing that I could hold my own
And sail to higher heights.

Maybe I would learn to strut
(Someone would tell me so).
Above my head, you just might see
A cute little gold halo.

I wonder if, then, I'd fix myself
When troubled, confused, or worn,
If I had been in charge myself
Before I was even born.

In that respect I guess it'd seem
My plans wouldn't be so bad—
With all my smart accomplishments,
Quite sure I'd be so glad.

But there's no other conclusion here.
If man attempts in part
To figure his own mortality,
He would fail to make a heart.

For the sovereignty of God alone
And whatever he has said
Would not have mattered in the
least
If man could look ahead.

Just another day to overthink
In a world occupied with sin,
I need not even waste the time
By imagining what might have
been.

The right things I should focused on,
Is affection I try to share,
I know God is a part of me
Because He's been right there.

I do not have to go way back
When my mother did conceive;
I only need to esteem my Lord—
And believe for what I need.

March 30, 2015

Happy Anniversary

I know that later Heaven will be the most
Magnificent place to be ...

but for now, living with you is!

Happy Anniversary!

June 10, 1974

Happy Anniversary, Pastor

Forty-four years is a long, long time
For anyone to be anywhere;
And forty-four years in one place
Means you really *have* to care.

Year after year we've come to say
How endearing a pastor you are,
To wish you grander times ahead
Than you have known thus far.

This time it's really special,
So all our greetings are such.
Rev. Stancil, we love you dearly.
We hope you know how much.

You're like the story of the kite
As it flew up out of sight.
We tugged the string, and you both were there;
Then we knew things were all right.

Feeling more contented—
For we too have long stood fast—
I trust that warmth from heart to heart
Will surely grow and last.

Well, being around so long a time,
Some things, no doubt, seemed hard;
But on the other hand, admit
It brought some great reward.

Though the body might get fragile
And the appetite's not so much,
You have to have a knowledge
The Lord knows how to touch.

So on this day—a glad event—
I pass to you this thought:
We all rejoice in the blessings
Shepherding forty-four years have brought.

April 22, 1992

Happy Birthday, Jerry

I've come to realize over all these years
We share a special bond,
So used to thinking much alike;
We call each other "hon."

You know I love you very much;
You hear it all the time.
I like to every now and then
Remind you in a rhyme.

All the things you do for me
To make me beam and smile;
You take good care of all my needs
And you do it with such style.

When you are happy, I am too,
That's just the way it is.
Happiness is actually sharing
And consoling each other's tears.

I sure do want to make this day
An exceptional one thus far;
The reason I'll always love you
Is because of who you are.

November 27, 1991

Happy Birthday with Love

I wanted to use fine words
That are suitable for me to say—
Not so much it's something new
In a peculiar sort of way.

Often a happy conclusion
Comes after a sour start;
It serves a need to express oneself
And leave a hidden heart.

Not too sure of what to do,
I've paced myself to crawl.
I focused on things that startled
When some aren't true at all.

But you and I went through
And passed a vital test;
We forged ahead to learn the good
And overlook the rest.

Things definitely aren't always planned;
Predicaments look bleak.
If everything went too well,
We wouldn't be strong but weak.

That's why we need to emphasize
How to value love and care;
That's something you can never buy—
Try searching everywhere.

No frowns, no remorse, no regrets,
No long face, and no pout—
It seems somewhat remarkable
It is without a doubt.

I'm excited to celebrate you,
Let's jump for joy and go,
We'll find a beautiful place to be
That no one else will know.

My life would sure be mixed up;
I'd be so incomplete.
My husband, I'd marry you over again
If sooner we could meet.

November 26, 1990

Happy Mother's Day, Mom

I was on my way last week
To buy a brand-new card;
To find one just appropriate
Should not have been so hard—

A Mother's Day greeting designed to say
Some things I might not can
And pretty pictures on the front
Like a pair of gentle hands,

A special card I'd notice
That was better than the others
Because it seemed a perfect fit
For my strong and marvelous mother.

But I considered option two
And try to express in part
My own attempt to write down
Some words inside my heart.

For I have lived a life unlike
Other children in this world,
Because I had the privilege
Of being your little girl.

Even if I'm not so small today,
Sweet memories still remain,
Repeating that I love you, Mom,
And that will stay the same.

April 29, 1991

Holy Father

To touch your threaded hem
Is my simple and long desire;
I want to feel your spirit
Soar up like raging fire.

In quiet, serene instances
Or when I wrench with tears,
I need you, Holy Father,
To calm my aches and fears.

So, so much gets fouled up.
Thus all I do is moan;
No, it's not a constant thing,
But I still feel so alone.

I recognize there is weakness.
Oh, my power seems to wane.
An issue has raised its ugly head,
So I face it once again.

But in spite of all confusions,
This one thing I can say:
No one but you, Almighty,
Can take it all away—

The fear of doubt and failure
Will be cast into the sea.
Praise God for revealing once again
Your grace is meant for me.

Thank you.

May 7, 1992

Honey

Honey, I might at any time
Want to just confess
I love you like I say I do,
Even more than you may guess.

And then again I love you
When I fail to let you know;
Sweetheart, you have a part of me
Everywhere that you may go.

You seem to think about me first
No matter what you do;
You always try your best to make
Some wish of mine come true.

But, darling, there are plenty of ways
My eyes have seen you love—
By being the guy who found me
And the man I'm so proud of.

You really do make me happy.
Don't let it slip *your* mind.
How can I help but smile toward you?
You've been so very kind.

My need of you is simply this:
Love me for myself.
If I didn't love you as I do,
There'd be nobody else.

February 2, 1972

Husband and Wife

Choosing to turn and
hurriedly flee
And wish this ache away,
I try to tune out sadness,
Not knowing quite what to say.

My desire, like yours, is
to settle this thing,
To stop discord and strife.
God didn't mean all this to be
Between a man and wife.

How easy the devil digs his claw
And squeezes our minds so tight.
It doesn't matter how long it takes;
He's prepared to stay all night.

It seems quite reasonable
what we do;
We justify how we act,
For all practical purposes
We speak those things *we* like.

What word, what
thought, what image
Is powerful to explain
How this irrational fiasco
Almost borders on insane?

If it's so easy to go round one,
To wrestle and win the fight,
To gather all our energies
And shore up all our might,

Then we are so deceived.
Our strength can't get us through.
We'd block out Holy Spirit;
He'd have very little to do.

But you and I both know inside
That no one wins this war,
And those we've brought
into this world
May stumble when going far.

If we'll not respect
each other's right
And purpose to exist,
How unfortunate to be alone
And regret the joy we've missed.

April 23, 1992

I Am Convinced

I'm truly convinced that in this time,
And I'm sure that through this day,
Favor will find and shadow me
In a divine and special way.

What a blessing to be aware,
That I'm privileged now to see,
I acknowledge his enormous awesomeness
Has nothing to do with *me*.

The only thing I know to do,
Even though I am just *one*,
Is to try to please my Master
So he will say, "Well done."

I want to reach a place in him,
A station I call elite.
Well, I can say I've found it—
It's simply at Jesus' feet!

September 14, 2015

I See You Understand

I personally want to thank you much.
Your gifts sure meant a lot.
You must've carefully considered me
And chose before you bought.

That means you kinda understood
What things I mostly like.
You picked out what is meaningful.
They were timely—they were right.

And the comments on my birthday card
Made for a special day.
I believe that we were bonding
In a uniquely special way.

So there's no more temptation
To hang my head and weep;
Unknowingly you gave me memories
That I should always keep.

July 14, 2015

I Will Love You Always, My Husband

Our separation hurts so much,
But the scriptures are true still:
Earth has no sorrow
That heaven cannot heal.
So I will just remember
And be honored to always say
I knew and loved my Jerry,
And that never goes away.
Whether "Father Time," "Pop," "Boss Man,"
Or other names that stand,
You were God-fearing, giving, and clever
And a truly Christian man.
Many already knew you were
Respected and so real.
You always worked and served
No matter what the deal.
We looked at you as quality,
An important reason why,
You developed with genuine love inside,
And that love will never die.
I am grateful for God's creation.
I was favored from above.
Oh Lord, it's hard to say so-long
To the easiest one to love.

June 14, 2014

I'm Sorry ... I'm Sorry

I mimic life on a splintered floor,
And I'm stuck in one more groove;
This pathetic emotion presented itself
And refused to quickly move.

I hope my mind's not inside out,
I did a thing quite wrong;
Even if I went there first,
I cannot stay too long.

And in so doing neither will hurt—
But give each other hope,
Making a day that's lovely,
And learn how we can cope.

Saying I'm sorry means nothing.
I've said it more than twice.
You forgave my stubborn self before
Because you are *that* nice.

Pardon my crude behavior,
Don't humble in defeat.
I don't deserve that gentleness;
You're too honorable and too sweet.

When will I finally realize
I'm living with my prince,
The one who truly loves me?
When will it make more sense?

Instead of trying to antagonize
On every little word,
Can I try to accept
The candid things I've heard?

I shouldn't try to pick through
Or to dissect each one by one;
I'm working on getting better in
My efforts to overcome.

It feels like time is fleeting fast
What time do I have left?
If my character shows damage from this,
No one's to blame but myself.

September 23, 1991

It Takes Time

One day I dreamed specifically
I'd set out on my mission;
I had to be there right on time
In order to clench my vision.

If I geared up for my conquest
And carefully dressed just so,
Opportunities would be incredible,
And up, up, and away I'd go.

Fortunately enough for me, though,
I arranged what cards were dealt.
I faced some unfair mocking
(They knew *not* how I felt).

Life's not fair is what I thought,
And in time it all came true.
Things unplanned can often say
What things we ought to do.

Funny, it's seldom timed just right.
We think we handle best.
Situations arise real fast
And entangle you in a mess.

But thanks to God there's promise.
We flourish because we can,
Taking time to believe it'll work—
Just follow the master plan.

The dealer may bluff if given a chance.
Don't allow the cards to fold.
Accept the fact that you can't know,
So don't think you're in control.

July 10, 1992

It's Not All Over

As my grateful heart was trained,
I didn't know myself
What it meant by ups and downs
How to change from right to left.
Of course I felt contented
In a world of lots unknown
On my way to experience life
As I called myself all grown.
I found myself wide-eyed,
Simple, young, and free;
Then I met my true beloved
Who desired to be with me.
I recognized what was happening
It was time for me to shift
And I needed to be my bravest;
I had waited for this gift.
Consistent years that followed,
What an honorable badge he wore
It got me more excited
And made me admire him more.
His lifetime and my years with him
God sanctioned and did allow.
Such a fulfilling life -- but tell me,
Oh Lord, my God ... what now?

June 30, 2014

It's Not Me That You See

I get many compliments lately,
Such welcome accolades,
From those who want to tell me
What growth in Christ I've made.

Some people didn't even know me
Two years or so ago,
But they simply say they notice
I've a certain kind of glow.

One reason is I am confident
With the time I may have left.
I've embraced more *who's* my strength,
And it's not rooted in myself.

Can I name one thing to boast?
Did I find some newfound wealth?
Has any great thing from me emerged
That I have done herself?

I pray that God does shine through me,
Even through my darkest night,
So *his* glory is what they really see—
Please help me live life right.

September 27, 2015

It's Not You

When a somber haze surrounds us,
Unplanned as it could be,
When the glimmer of the day gets dark,
It's really not you—it's me.

If great powers lit the entire world
So perceptive minds could see,
I'd probably still be impetuous …
It's really not you—it's me.

From in my heart it all seems right;
What I give to you is free:
A sparkle to make that smile appear.
It is not you —it's me.

You're so concerned with what I want,
Expressed by you sincerely.
My spirit can't help but agree with yours.
You're the reason, my dear—not me.

June 8, 1992

Jeanette

An abundance of Grace we receive from God …
On our face he gives a kiss,
So when we think of mates gone on,
He fills those moments we miss.

Whatever our plight throughout this life,
What plan our Savior has,
You and I can rest assured
His abiding love will last!

I dare not forget to give him praise
For all that he has done,
And against the evil that roams around …
God has already won!

As you experience this time (second year),
Brother Mitch is stationed up high.
He's sending a special smile to you,
But he can't ever cry

Because there are no tears up there.
Glorious heaven is such a place,
And that is where we'll long to be
When we finish *our* journey's race.

No matter how frail you sometimes get,
Remember you had a friend.
May God reward your caring heart
When you see Mitch in the end!

February 12, 2014

Jesus

The Jesus whom I know is real;
He's not a lifeless object.
He's done so much for me that now
He is my special subject.

I want to write about his works;
I want to praise his name—
To let you know that from the start
He's always been the same.

Whatever may unfold in times
Of sadness and distress,
The Savior is a comforter and
The one who gives me rest.

He knows exactly what I feel
And is concerned with every need;
The key is faith—and it will grow;
Just plant and water seed.

I cannot be convinced at all,
There're limits our hearts can hold.
So prepare to experience happiness
That the years have seen untold.

I trust the Lord to hold me
No matter what I do.
If I carry my petitions to God in prayer,
I know He'll see me through.

Whether there's difficulty in finance
Or pain has slowed me down,
I just look up to him for help;
He's always close around.

I pray He'll give me favor.
As I serve him true and meek
So I may one day wear my crown
In glory that I seek.

I know the Lord protects me
Through paths of risk and harm;
When the way becomes quite chilly,
His love will wrap me warm.

I hope I have not failed to show
What godly thoughts can mean;
I just don't plan to fall apart—
Upon his Word I lean.

Halleluiah! Thank you, Lord,
You made my vision bright.
No matter what—no matter what—
You will make all things all right.

January 21, 1971

Joy to the World

Joy to the world and peace on earth—
The season's here once more.
It's still a festive time of year
Without snow by every door.

There is a surefire way, you see,
To deliver a warming smile.
Just set aside next Friday
For brunch and relax a while.

With covered dishes and knick-knacks,
With sweets and salads and drink,
We could party in our break room.
A good idea, you think?

No matter if you cook or not,
There are other people who do;
We'll decide what to bring right now
So the planning is all but through.

Mingle a while, coworkers,
Display some holiday cheer.
Lord knows what else we'll contend with
Come the month of December next year.

December 13, 1990

Just Staying Faithful

I may have been in a pickle—
Didn't know to what extent.
Just couldn't rightly figure out
What all these issues meant.

I'm confident I was acting nice,
My disposition unchanged.
Don't remember what I did so bad,
Thought life was all arranged.

Then all at once I found myself
Scratching my head, amazed.
Where is all this madness from
That left me bruised and dazed?

I had prepared to move away
And start my saintly walk,
Secure that I was reaching up
To a height where I might talk.

My communication
would be inspiring;
People would want to grow.
I'd impress with proper clothing
And be prominent high and low.

Oh, my God, I prayed to know
How I could face this test.
Why did that thing I
thought was right
Connect to all this mess?

In what struggles I
must go through,
I pray my faith will be
Strong enough along the way
For him to rescue me.

I may not yet have answers,
And fears sometimes can rise,
But I pledge to still be faithful.
God's mercy is no surprise.

July 15, 2015

Keeping My Head

I used to try much harder
To keep myself in line,
But lately I've been slipping up;
I've gotten a bit behind.

Whenever I try to get where I
Just really plain don't care,
The consequence is problems
So very hard to bear.

So just this once I thought
I'd chat about it some;
Talking just to me right now
Can't do me any harm.

What's my thing? What's happening
here?
Why this hurt and grief?
What's the complaining all about?
Exactly what's my beef?

To be perfectly honest,
I wish I knew myself;
It's hard to recognize reasons
For unpleasant things I've felt.

And just think: so many times
Thoughts were carefree and sweet;
I could give a hasty smile
To everyone I'd meet.

I thought I was an okay miss;
I wasn't all that bad.
Eventually I'd make up for
Any flaws I may have had.

But looks like now it's different;
There's been a delicate change.
Now some things I always do
Just seem so very strange.

Am I purposely trying
To do things that aren't right?
Why do I make the day so dark
That others make so bright?

I wish there was an easier way
To fight this grip on me—
To try to watch my temperament
And restrain it secretly.

What makes it worse is the fact
That I know it's wrong to start,
But yet it's hard to reason
Before I close my heart.

I must remember those many times
Of actions in the past;
I must recall such a thought
Was never meant to last.

I must try to do daily
Somebody some kind of good;
I must fulfill those things in life
I know for sure I should.

I must start now to do this;
I have no time to rest.
I cannot do it on my own,
But with God I'll pass this test.

January 28 and January 29, 1971

Lessons

People come and people go to heights they feel their aim;
Realize, though, that in truth, some see it as a game.
    Might be a win; might be a loss.
    But somebody had to pay that cost.
Let's not forget some lessons remain.

Haven't you heard that we're at war?
So we're praying for miracles near and far.
    Some people are perturbed when they
    Can't manage to figure a better way
To find out where some sinless places are.

They're smart, somewhat, and patient—yes,
Striving dearly to do their best.
    I sympathize with how they feel,
But it will require God's perfect will
When we finish taking this lifelong test.

Christ has already paid that price—believe.
The power of his blood is what we need
    No matter the wrongs we may have done;
    Repenting for them means we have won.
Praise God in whom we move and breathe.

June 29, 1972

Lingering Love

Even when it's light of day
I remember the night before,
I cannot seem to help but smile,
As I exit out my door.

I head out for my work day
No rush – I'll get there when
I recall how beautiful it was with you
And I manage to smile again.

The day will surely drag on
But that's okay .. I've learned
How again to feel that lingering love
As soon as I return.

June 30, 1971

Living for Jesus

When night has come and day has gone,
I often wonder when
We'll obey what he commands
And lasting peace begin.

I may not have a brilliant mind
Or have a gorgeous face.
I'm sure not very famous
And outstanding among my race.

I might just have a shabby car,
Barely enough for it to pass.
If judged on shapely figures,
I might place next to last.

What things I should be focused on
As I look high up above,
I'm learning there is no substitute,
For a heart that's full of love.

Like I say, I'm not so smart,
And I'm recognized by few,
But if I had authority,
This is what I'd do:

Help everyone to realize
That faith, forgiving, and trust
Come through God, and all is good
For every one of us.

Let's share the things we want to have
So together we all can live.
Tell someone else He'll fix each thing
No matter what it is.

August 25, 1971

Long Ago

It seems like so long ago
When we went different ways.
It seems more like several years
And not just several days.

I touched your hand, you touched my lips,,
We took the time to share,
Exchanging only simple words
To say we truly care.

Thinking again how great it is
That I can write and say
I offer from me to you right now
In my very special way.

You may not know but tried to guess
Exactly how I feel,
I'm trying to show I've got your back,
Do you think I ever will?

I've tried to write about it;
I've tried to say it plain.
But if it comes out a little jumbled,
I'm looking at you the same.

I don't intend to give up ever.
It would be a terrible bet.
Why should I plan on starting now
When I haven't started yet?

To make this story short and sweet,
I'd like to let you know,
Believe your wife when she says out loud,
"Sweetheart, I love you so."

January 8, 1971

Loving Thoughts

I touched my face, now wet with tears—
Didn't even realize why.
I told myself at start of day
It's way too soon to cry.

All I tried to accomplish
Was to get beyond this road
Step by step and day by day
Underneath this heavy load.

I thought some song would do the trick
Or a memory I remembered when
A face adored me;
May I feel adored again?

Strange—it worked a little bit.
The words and beat implied
I still had *something* going on,
Despite my calm disguise.

So now I'll turn the music down
And realize I am good.
Songs can't love the way God does.
Oh my, I wish they could!

August 4, 2015

Mama Says: Look Up, My Daughter

In honor of this wedding day,
Though it's not easy to express
The abundant love inside this place,
Share a thousand words or less—

It's like a knowing thread of warmth
That connects to all who feel.
Your daddy's heart's all over you,
And he says he loves you still.

You picked this special date and time
To show this special crowd
You'll always be your daddy's girl,
And he's so very proud.

He's watching over his baby grown up,
And yes, some tears were wept.
He said he'd always love you, Sam;
That's a promise he made and kept.

What's more befitting November 28
As you make your vows and smile.
His loving spirit is by your side
As you gracefully walk the aisle.

On daddy's special birthday,
What we'd give to just once more
Run joyfully up to greet him
As he stands there at the door.

But for those who really knew him,
You know he'd want to say,
"Y'all, go ahead and *celebrate*
On this wonderful, wonderful day."

He'd tell you don't be sad for him.
He's in heaven—and he'll see.
You deserve a perfect wedding day,
And he's as proud as he can be!

November 27, 2014

More Than Ever

I don't know of ways enough
To show the fondness I feel,
To prove you're in my heart, dear one,
And stay you always will.

I haven't achieved the talents yet
To draw a picture of such,
To make it crystal clear to all,
To show you're loved so much.

If my words would somehow do the job
Of assuring you I care,
I'd be among the famous
Speakers anywhere.

I didn't really relate too well;
I only gave a hint
Of the pleasure I get from the things you do,
What closeness truly meant.

But if you haven't learned by now
Or the fact has slipped your mind,
Just let me help you remember
By saying one more time.

If I had it to do all over again,
I can't imagine why
I'd want to change a single thing
Or even want to try.

Because I think the world of you,
From your whisper to your touch;
I'm the proudest wife on God's green earth
If you love me half as much.

April 22, 1971

Mother's Thank-You

It really takes no grand affair
On the second week in May—
A pretty dress and done-up hair
To prepare for church that day.

If just for this special time,
No cooking and no concerns,
Enjoy all the accolades
Of what you think you've earned.

The yesteryears don't matter now;
Different days for us just *were*.
And never mind the trials to come—
Stay strong when they occur.

For now (this day) with what it is,
We face some cruel attacks,
But what this good life brought to me—
I would never give it back!

Why? Because I'm pleased …
As Mother, that's what I do.
I'm honored and I'm favored
To mother the three of you.

Oh how I want to tell you girls
(And your dad does take a part)
Y'all are responsible for giving me
A warmth within my heart.

My dears … any time you have a day
When it's dim and hard to see,
What you do is breathe a smile
And take a look at me.

Love always … Mom.

April 10, 2012

My Borrowed Children

When my children dashed outside,
I would cry …
They ran splendid and swift,
Enjoying an unpretentious lift;
Let's pray their spirits don't die!

I asked at their very birth
That they might bid farewell
To the ugliness of early hell
And repression in the earth.

My babes in arms, gentle and sweet—
Fresh-opened lips and eyes peer
At this alien face drawn so near
But yearn for our touch to meet.

Our hearts must utterly bind.
O Lord, please make me wise
And help me stop any hurtful guise;
Compel me to waste no time.

I don't own anything myself,
But for a while, I am quite sure,
What I borrow is close to pure
Through the love my child has left.

I'll not complain in raggedy shoes,
For I am content in knowing
My babies are sweetly growing,
With love they'll never lose.

September 4, 1991

My Christmas of Love

The thought that came to mind today,
Has bloomed into a song,
A pleasurable rhythm to remind me of
How affection with time has grown.

Because you're one of very few
Whose kindness just rushed on through,
It revealed to me and convinced me
Of the honest-to-goodness you.

This Christmas season I want to give
A token of my love
To thank you for what you've been
Through the spirit up above.

Although God's love is superior
To what we humans conceive,
My love for you is growing warm
Each day I live and breathe.

My dear, it means so much to me
I'm tempted to say it twice—
For understanding who I was
And for being so very nice.

So nothing really fancy, hon,
And nothing I do so smart—
Just a gift of love (for always)
From the bottom of my heart.

December 23, 1971

My Dark Days

Even darkest days should have some light.
I only ask, am I all right?
Will God see fit to touch me still
And show me of his perfect will?
There must be more to life than this;
I long too much for times I've missed.
I'm misty as I watch the moon.
Am I desiring to maneuverer too soon?
The good fruit on my tree can't drop
Claim me before my flowering will stop.

July 7, 2015

My Dear Kim

It was only for a short, short time
You were able to gently touch
Your premature and precious boy,
But you cherished him oh so much.

He gave mother something special
As you held him for a while,
A bundle of only innocence
That was wrapped up with his smile.

The scripture says to bless the Lord
And his benefits don't forget.
Though our hearts cry out for Carter now,
He *existed* ... and so yall met.

So as I try to find the words
And petition to God above,
Please be a comfort to my friend Kim —
As I send to her my love.

September 11, 2015

My Girls

All the things I've said thus far
Throughout your growing years
Were meant to try to spare you from
Many pointless pains and tears.

You girls mean the world to me,
And as hard as I tried to be
The right kind of mother/friend
To you deserving three,

I still don't get complacent,
Because I know it's true
You may depend on me for stuff
But I need you, darlings, too.

Experience comes a lot with age,
Or at least that's what I'm told,
But grasping values and character
Happens long before we're old.

And that is why I've attempted
To inspire, to encourage, to instill
That when relating your worth to others
It's okay to show you're real.

Through all your life assignments
And all the tasks and fun,
Whenever you need a caring heart,
There will at least be one.

July 9, 1992

My Heart Hurts

I thought I had a surefire way
To soar above that storm.
That sudden separation
Has caused me so much harm.

It was timed that it should happen,
But had I noticed it near,
I think I might have done *something*
Without adding to the fear.

For after all I'm sharp enough—
I could've used my head
To figure out a strategy
Just like the doctor said.

But I must have missed a vital part
Where he suggested what to do.
I'm angry ... didn't he understand
It affected everyone but you?

I lost the person who knew me
Just like I knew myself—
Did he realize he was leaving
So he prepared before he left?

I'm trying very hard to slow my cry
And be mindful whom I had.
It's just not easy to soothe my heart,
Because it hurts so bad.

August 15, 2015

My Hope ...

One day God chose to enlighten me
That *I* wouldn't see the end,
He allowed me to be reconciled ...
And introduced me as a friend.

He reminded me that along the way
I dare not attempt to face
The harshness of reality
Without his love and grace.

"Where is your answer?" I asked.
"Does it matter looks and charm?
I'm listening, God," to which he said,
"Just lean upon my arm."

So I'm learning to do the best I can.
I try daily to abide.
Whatever I need and do not have,
Those things he will provide.

You know—I know—we share a past
Though we live our lives apart.
I hope that in this small, small way
I'm touching your natural heart.

June 29, 2015

My Life

My life is really good thus far
No matter how time will flow,
I'm fitted with my special shoes
There's a way I must now go.

I follow patterns, yes,
Compelled to brave it through,
But *I* must be creative—
In what I need to do.

Guide me constantly, guide me
I want to stand up strong,
I'll never totally be miss right,
Sometimes I'll be so wrong.

Often I look toward others
To live some portion of my life.
Oh silly me!
There is no duplicate of me!

I must live my life as best I can,
For my life has not preceded me.

July 10, 1971

My Petition … My Plea

I petition consistently to God (our God),
And I wanted you to know
I pray for *special* care to you
Wherever you have to go.

Keep that heart …you've prayed so long
For those who lay in bed.
Inviting the sweet and Holy Spirit
Who has already gone ahead.

May your going out and coming in
Be blessed each mile you tread,
For God will bless and keep you
Isn't that just what he said?

For burdens aren't brought by Jesus.
Other people may never see.
I'm praying God stays gracious
As he hears my constant plea.

April 15, 2015

My Savior ... My Lord

I want to lift your holy name,
For all you say is true.
As I humbly kneel to thee,
I desire to honor you!

All the while you've been my strength.
You've not hid after all;
It's just sometimes *my* eyes are shut
As I try hard not to fall.

You have touched me ... yes, you have,
And you've helped me to endure
What things I've dealt with lately,
But my thoughts still seem unsure.

Deliver me from my doubting,
From confusion, and from fear.
Even in my brokenness,
I'll acknowledge that you're right here.

I want a boldness that supersedes—
That grows with love no less.
I desire a passing grade from you,
'Cause it's near my time to test.

Bless me, Lord, abundantly
In what things I need to do.
Water my seeds of service
That they grow to please just you!

There's much, too much, you've done for me,
A raggedy form of self.
If you even look away from me,
Surely nothing at all is left.

While I seek and claim your benefits,
I'm glad some things occurred.
Whatever glory it gives you,
I'll be grounded in your Word.

June 2, 2015

Mystic

To admire the one who discovered me
Is indeed something rare.
Would you just stay for always
If I whispered it in prayer?

Would your eyes behold me warmly
As you took your time and spoke?
Would your arms be ample strong enough
To surround me when I woke?

Right this moment when I wish to feel
Your heart upon my own,
Could I linger there for just a while —
Could I rest where I belong?

Often I get emotional,
But you don't need to guess;
It's okay to connect with me, my love,
And put your mind at rest.

Hold tight when I'm mysterious;
We've got so much ahead.
Some people waste such precious time.
Let's snatch it up instead.

If I travel miles away,
If I wade the river wide,
I know you make me capable,
For I'll have your love inside.

May 5, 1971

Needs

We're not here living life
Because of all our beauty.
We're not even needed
To accomplish some sense of duty.

Tomorrow we could wake up
But not be able to hear,
Or speak, or smell, or see anything.
(Oh, what a thing to fear!)

Our riches don't really matter
To anyone but ourselves;
If God would stop his mercy,
What other life is left?

Any vain and selfish motives
Uncover an attitude
Of indifference and uncaring
And we act downright rude.

If I don't drive a fancy car
Or dress in fashion's best;
What if my brother's trousers
Aren't so very neatly pressed.

Yeah, I pick up aluminum cans
Every chance I get,
Get caught in rain at bus stops,
And get home soaking wet.

I may have to borrow
Before the end of month,
Trying to stretch five dollars
To at least buy bread and punch.

Sometimes I need to cry
Though I know things aren't
that bad;
My tide will come back one day soon,
And I'll laugh at troubles had.

But if I had to have my way,
I'd want to make quite sure
To keep in mind what's vital,
To value things that are pure.

Allow God first to use my hands,
Maintaining humbleness
To be and do all that I can
And let him do the rest.

God knows I need finances.
He knows just where and when,
I trust He'll give me sufficient,
And uplift me once again.

When I come into my riches,
I'll spare more than a dime;
To witness about God's goodness
Is how I'll use my time.

July 18, 1991

Our Precious Little Girl

Does a rose sweetly blossom
When it's happy and content?
Does a baby pup remember
What his mama's touch has meant?

Does the robin spread its wings aloft
When soaring far and wide?
Does the mother duck keep watch
Over her duckling by her side?

As if there weren't enough of all
This beauty in the world,
The Lord sent from heaven
Our precious little girl.

Mama and Dad's little angel joy,
So tiny yet so dear,
You always shall be loved so much
As long as we are here.

Although to teach you right from wrong
Will surely be a task,
With such a lovely daughter,
What more could parents ask?

July 14, 1971

Praise the Lord!

So many types of gardens in life,
And we think the choice is ours;
Do we sometimes pick a thorn
And miss the sweetest flower?

Our destiny permits our decisions.
Whether we realize it to be
Wisdom from things experienced,
I pray we all will see.

I've come to know there's hope!
There's a greater power yet near;
We can shoulder so much we
thought not
And rejoice even with a tear.

I think tears are part of strength.
That's what God needs from us—
Not a conflict or discouragement
But a binding heart to trust.

He wants each and every one
To accept his word as true;
No promise of his ever failed
In all the years gone through.

I tell you it's a privilege.
Really, where would we now be?
Without the risen Savior,
The man from Galilee?

Oh, it's not a fiction tale;
Story for real took place,
Christ suffered for us and died
And on the third day was raised.

Yes, that day he suffered,
So dark and filled with gloom,
But he sacrificed his blood for us;
He prepared in Heaven more room.

Not that we'll ever deserve him,
In *human* terms we're lost;
But praise the Lord he fixed that
When he died upon that cross.

Jesus showed love in action,
That's reason we live to say,
Thank you, Lord, for everything.
It's your joy that fills my day.

April 1, 1971

Proud Wife

Wonderful were the days we shared,
And joy more days will bring.
Upon your head is not a crown,
But you remind me of a king.

It appears I love you dearer
When time has come between;
I cherish lots more the knowledge of what
A loving family means.

I cannot help but try
To just say in part
Words to express I'm proud to have
A place within your heart.

No matter how much I repeat myself
Or how simply the phrases rhyme,
The important thing is I'll love you
Throughout your life and mine.

Years will change a lot of things;
No exception is made for us.
But at least we know the good will reign
From our closeness, respect and trust.

To only let our spirits touch,
With whispers sounding sweet,
I send my love as best I know
Till again we both shall meet.

Though I may have said it times before,
Again is kind of nice;
No doubt you're all the husband
I will ever want in life.

June 30, 1971

Pursuing Your Righteousness

Besides my Lord, no savior exists,
The scripture reads today.
So pursuing his righteous wisdom
Is what I do—I pray.

I crave to truly set my mind
On things far up above.
Then I can't miss exposing
That God is purely love.

Can it be when I've done *that*
Do I dare to shrink and hide?
Not when he truly loves me,
And saw my heart inside.

My spirit desires a fullness.
I beg not to be slack.
When life tries to trip me up,
Please Lord, just have my back.

July 14, 2015

Rage

So what do I do the next time
That broken record plays—
The old one where I yell
And fall into a daze?

I don't so much fly off the handle
And lose my sense of fair,
It's just not very believable
That people do really care.

Some unplanned things will floor you
Little situations do arise;
I'll need to watch and pray, I suppose,
Then it's not a real surprise.

September 23, 1991

Reflections and Tribute from the Family
For Granddear

A part of us is crying out,
Consoling and holding tight.
With all the happy memories
We should cling with all our might.

Sharing, caring like families do,
And alike in that it seemed
Nothing for long would separate
The things we always dreamed.

We knew all was not perfect,
But we cherished her strength in life,
For Robbie was a sweetheart,
Not only mom and wife.

Thank you, Lord, for making her,
For gifting her within.
We'll always have her smile with us;
She was the dearest friend.

We can't evade a sad, sad heart.
The bruising darts have flown,
But we truly have your comfort
And we're not left alone.

Inside our soul and conscience
Is knowledge that we've had
A wonderful life with Granddear,
And we are more than glad.

It's now our time to say good-bye.
Lord, help us see our way.
She was such a special lady,
And we'll meet again one day.

June 25, 1995

Remember Love

There are rewards I am entitled to
If I manage to hold on tight,
Because I can remember
That love is always right.

At times my raw emotions
Could begin when he walked by,
Or as I rested next to him
It could almost make me cry.

My ear could feel his beating heart
As I cuddled on his chest.
I wanted to only think on him,
For I didn't need much rest.

Connecting beneath or on the top
With no expected plan,
Bonding true affections
So the other would understand …

That taking the time to give love back
Would make each one feel whole.
That's the love I remember well.
May it always soothe my soul.

August 25, 2015

Salty Tears

The richness of your love is peace.
I'm glad that I can find
Your guiding truth above all else
To saturate my mind.

That truth being *you're* God alone.
All wisdom you possess.
You said you'd never forsake me,
Lord.
I'll pray to believe no less.

For I am learning where to get
The answers to my fears;
Whenever I struggle and have to cry
You feel my salty tears.

All I ask for you to do
Is, really, what you have done,
My very best praise is thanking you
For steering me on this run.

If there's a thing inside of me
That grieves you from this day,
Please, please, please remove it.
I pray your will … your way.

Give me strength and soothe me
Hear my humble cry.
You've been so very good to me,
Sometimes I wonder why.

As I am blessed to call your name,
Gazing high to you above,
I utter a prayer of gratitude
From a heart that's full of love.

July 12, 2015

Sammie

A child's disobedience
Can be tough enough to take;
You sometimes get an urge
To toss him in the lake.

But that innocence makes you patient,
And you overlook some deed.
Like generals in a war zone,
We're to do our job and lead.

Child didn't ask to come here,
But I welcome those little feet.
Just to hold this little one
For me is such a treat!

December 13, 1991

Seeking God's Face

Surely my God is in this place,
For he has snatched my frown.
He's showing me *he* is beautiful …
If only I look around.

He's not about to throw me back
Because I tripped and fell,
But he allows my rescue
Through stories I'm blessed to tell.

I want so much to reverence him.
It's a joy that holds me safe.
He's reached down with his open hand;
That's what I chose to take.

I have a journey to travel now.
I decided at start of race
Not lose my sight of him out front
As I bow and seek his face.

July 11, 2015

Sister

Does it matter what I say right now?
Can I erase the recent past?
Can a simple life be mended
And sisters be close at last?

If we could utter now somehow
What we couldn't utter then,
Could we at least admit
It hurts to lose a friend?

I'm realizing there's a spirit
That drives a heated mind.
It circles *any* negative
And attacks the good and kind.

It carries away any common sense
From whatever place we're at,
And it does not have intentions
To quiet a tit for tat.

We've seen it happen times before
On a job or in a car.
It can rear its ugly head so quick
And it lingers not too far.

But as far as I'm concerned today,
No reason to extend that fight.
I've invited the Lord to dwell in us
And to make everything all right.

July 25, 2015

So Alone

Nothing to reach for next to me,
I'm ready for the taking …
There is no longing
now *toward* me;
Will I ever stop this shaking?

I haven't had time to really dream
'Cause it doesn't seem all real.
For what purpose did
I come this way?
Why was my world made still?

I cannot recall the last time
I felt my body sweat—
Not special like it used to be.
Well, that's long gone, I bet.

Now in this place I sit and think
As I stare beyond the lake.
Convince me I am worthy;
How long will all this take?

I haven't been able to comprehend
How you mend a tiny part
Of a heart so big, but wounded
Where do I even start?

Tell me where it's written down
I must hold on tight for years?
There's abundant love inside of me
That *blinds* my eyes with tears?

Emotions can swell up suddenly.
I expect that pretty much,
But I remember
embraces helped …
Oh, it felt so good to touch.

Who values my existence now?
Do I surrender or try to fight?
I thirst for God's assurance
As I face this lonely night.

April 19, 2015

Speak, Lord

In reading and studying this early morn
And praying that I might see,
I turned first to a calendar thought
In First Samuel chapter 3.

It spoke of spending listening time
To fully be aware
That God wants to remind me
That he is always there.

"Speak, Lord," is what the prophet prayed,
For this boy didn't know at first
That God was speaking to *his* heart
With a loud, anointed word.

However many times it actually took
For Samuel to hear it clear,
He did not have an attitude
Like some of us have here.

Try saying, "Speak, Lord. I'll listen,"
But we say, "Listen, God. I'll speak."
Could that just be a cause
We miss the answer we seek?

My prayer and my desire is
Holy Spirit, keep me strong.
I want to live sincerely right.
Will you love me if I'm wrong?

August 12, 2015

Starting Anew

I believe I want to face the truth,
To know without a doubt
I don't have to be unkind.
So what's this all about?

I've studied too long being hurt.
Now I've become aware
The core of what's inside of me
Knows earnestly how to care.

Yes, I perceive I'm ready enough
To admit there're things I lack.
Used to have resilience, but
Can I ever get that back?

I don't desire to be alone
With a trembling in my heart.
Cast me not as star on stage,
I do not fit that part.

I crave to be more confident
In what I'm led to do,
Don't purposely want to wound you
As I start this journey new.

August 14, 2015

Staying Humble

Yes, I heard your compliments,
And it gave me such a spark.
It really lit me up inside,
As my moments sometime get dark.

It made me once again recall
What other things you've said.
You even shared a verse or two
Of poetry you had read.

"You look very nice today." You smiled,
And you didn't bat an eye.
"You are a shining light to me"
(Oh, you almost made me cry.)

The one thing I'm both glad and sad
Is that I respect you too;
I'm waiting for this all to cease,
And I'll start so missing you.

I am not able to command what's next,
But this I'll pledge to do,
I will stay in truth and humbleness;
When it relates from me to you.

March 30, 2015

Survival

Life and fiction are blended
When a tragedy is close at hand.
Images are distinctly different
But not easy to understand.

With eyes wide open to see it
And teeth clenched ever tight,
It's really all we can do
To prepare ourselves to fight.

What the world to us has offered
Is not always a deal;
It leaves out reasons to transform
For the way we sometimes feel.

It's based on certain conditions,
We can choose to accept its cost
It may turn out to be a win,
Or quite possibly be a lost.

I met an old, survival friend.
It was good to talk a while;
It was safe to see another face
Not afraid at all to smile.

When I cheerfully returned the favor,
At that moment could forget
The chaos and confusion
And all the other mess.

I remembered my choice to spend that time
Not focusing on the least
But seeing again what love looks like,
Ah, it brought me welcomed peace.

July 15, 1992

Thank You for Your Gift

Father, you are the author.
You are finisher to end of time.
You show up in my every day.
You're mighty, and you're kind.

I lift up both my hands to you.
I pray that they are clean.
May I reflect what you instilled
A thirst for love, not mean.

I think back and remember you
On the day that I was birthed.
Did I thank you for my mother
Who carried me on this earth?

I understand she suffered pains,
And almost died, you see,
But you were there to cover her;
So, too, you shielded me.

Else I never would have known
A mother's love this life.
Oh, praise you for that gift you gave.
Again you paid that price.

I thank you for your everything.
I pray that all I do
Will convey to others humbly
That they can have it, too.

July 16, 2015

Thank You for Your Kind Words

I would not try to figure out
Or at all try to guess
The number of eulogies you have
done …
I'll just say this was your best.

Reverend, when I walked inside
New Bethel yesterday
I saw my dad stretched out in front.
I wondered what words you'd say.

It wasn't long before I heard
The songs expressed with joy
And words on the life of Stephen
Ever since he was a boy.

And though Dad wasn't young in age,
You knew he's from good stock,
How else could he have survived
like that
But by standing on the Rock?

The connection you wisely put
together
With what this man had been—
Reverend Webb, you sounded close
enough
To really be next of kin.

Nothing at all I thought of
Was missing from this story.
I'm truly confident, as you said,
Dad's resting up in glory.

I think my husband might be one
Assigned to his grand tour
As they walk on streets of gold
Rejoicing with praise, I'm sure.

So please accept this thank-you, sir.
You laid out all the parts
Of eulogizing brilliantly
And lifting up all our hearts.

October 26, 2014

That Someone Is You

The tears I shed are not because
I feel so sad and blue;
They fall because I'm happy that
I share my life with you.

Because I just cannot imagine
The thought of being here
Without that someone precious
And lovable and dear.

That someone who has always tried
To do his best indeed,
Hoping to be with me
Or available in times of need.

That someone whom I speak of
Makes many of my dreams seem real;
He surely must be a reason
For delightfulness I feel.

All the time we spent alone,
The time we spent apart,
I know how much the simple things
Have deepened in my heart.

I think it's time I shouted out
Just who that someone is,
I figure you have figured out
Who makes me smile through tears.

You can be most charming,
Allow me to be true;
That someone I'm in love with
Is no one else but you.

January 11, 1971

The Bathroom Mirror

The mirror above my
bathroom sink
Wasn't big or wide enough
To show just what was going on
In dealing with all my stuff.

I tried to crack a trembling smile
With no one there to see;
It was hard for me to recognize
What thing I am to be.

My eyes were blurred and puffy.
My cheeks had dried-up tears,
And the softness in
this rounded face
Showed changes
throughout the years.

I remembered to say my
thankful prayer
At the beginning of the day.
I said, God, I'm so grateful …
Would you guide me in your way?

I asked would he prepare me,
Would he confirm his Word inside?
I need that intimate Comforter
To be my constant guide.

Can I still learn your counsel?
(Has it made a little dent?)
I'm praying and I expect, my Lord:
Please renew my fragile strength.

For I can't explain my
brand-new pains
I do the best I can.
I offer my own conjectures,
But will you understand?

The little things or the big things,
It's all the same to you,
Remind me as I go forth now
You're there to guide me through.

No, my mirror cannot talk back,
But the Spirit reveals *I'm kept*.
His hand of mercy still holds me,
And he's every bit my help.

July 6, 2015

The Lord's Hand

In whose hands we give our fragile hearts,
Praying we're poised for love to start.
Giving thanks for blessings done,
May we just try to be as one.
So many things we often do
That don't include a part of you;
So focused on what the others may say,
Or dictate if to live the right way—
To be overly kind, to work extra fast
As if this moment might be our last.
Such a beautiful time for each to share
The peace to know that we can care,
Assurance within to say, "indeed,
The Lord shall supply my every need."
No wavering faith, but in true belief,
Whether happiness and joy, or sadness and grief.
If he never choses to bless us again,
We think how good the Lord's really been.
Pity, some may soon forget
We really aren't deserving—ah, but yet
God's grace has sustained as lives unfold.
His enlightened words shall not grow old.
Let's try to *be* Love a lifetime longer.
The Lord is quite able to help us be stronger.

February 7, 1978

The Workplace

I woke before the clock alarmed,
Just had things on my mind;
I'd get an early start, I thought,
But still was running behind.

The car brakes squeaked as usual,
And the radio played hit tunes,
But I feared I might not make it—
I was barely riding on fumes.

So I got to work in a hurry.
I had no time to waste;
One almost has to arrive by six
For a decent parking space.

The stress had started to worsen;
My mind was being coerced.
But I didn't fret too long, because
I knew how much it's worth.

The day will linger long
If moods are dim and low;
I decided to give little fuzzies
As the day went to and fro.

For no matter who or where we are,
We can try to share a smile;
The secret is in remembering
The things that are worthwhile.

December 12, 1991

This Day

Before the sun shall show its face
And before the phone can ring,
I want to rest and fully know
I have worshiped and praised my King.

Did I recognize that you were there
When I breathed in with my breath?
Did I bless someone in passing by
By smiling before I left?

Was I really even conscience
When I began to do my fast?
Did I acknowledge again your sacrifice?
Did you keep me from a crash?

You deserve so much, my Father,
I shout to you and say
How good you've constantly been to me—
May I thank you for this day.

July 13, 2015

This Lasting Moment

I sit and try to think of words
To say at times like this,
Recalling all the chances
Of loving you I've missed.

I can't do much about that now,
But I can really try
To share my deep affection
Until we say good-bye.

For once we say good-bye once more,
I hope we won't again,
Just hold me tight and squeeze me
And take my trembling hand.

Tell me that you care for me
Through your sweet and gentle touch;
Help me feel more reassured
I need not worry much.

For whatever happens, come what may,
At least I have this thought:
I found exactly the character
And the quality things I've sought.

I adore you, and its genuine;
It'll live on when I die,
I trust you receive what I can give
Then you will feel as I.

Things that mean the world to us
Have only just begun;
Let's show the ones who may have doubts,
That you and I are one.

January 18, 1971

This Race

There's a way that seems so comfy,
A road where little is dread.
Others can offer you plenty of props
Down that crowded path ahead.

You might be tempted to shin and grin
With a body young and strong.
Maybe you even think sometimes,
That you can do no wrong.

Then out of the blue, on one fine day,
No clouds above at all,
You'll accidently stumble,
And take a sudden fall.

Of course, you get all wounded
And others taunt and jeer.
You quickly try to compose yourself,
For your finish is nowhere near.

Your dried-out mouth needs quenching.
Ah, a little water … you sipped.
Did you see just *where* you fell down?
And *why* was it you tripped?

It's not about you, remember that.
Better focus on his face,
The way to assuredly get that prize
Just obey him on this race.

August 27, 2015

To Jerry

It may not be all necessary
  To write each other notes;
    In fact, it's probably rare these days
      Among us age-able folks.

There are unkind things we'll remember
  If we live back in the past,
    But within that scope we lived to see,
      Those troubles didn't really last.

So I thought I'd write a poem to you;
  Today it just seems right.
    Welcome home … my husband dear,
      We'll be as one tonight.

And when you have to leave again
  And face what things you face,
    Know back home you're guaranteed
      To have a special place.

February 3, 2014

To Love and Be Loved

Oh yes, I'm strong ... I've said it now,
No hiding because I'm weak,
I face myself in such a place
When the world is dark and bleak?

I claimed to see my target clear,
But my aim was off ... I missed,
I'd better look around again
And make a brand new list.

I wrote my dreams from yesteryear
And marked the ones not reached,
Like one where we're hand in hand
As we walk along the beach.

How 'bout the one that promised me
Today I'd meet a friend;
I thought if two became just one
It'd be until the end.

I dreamed that I *could* shed my tears
And you would understand,
That you'd be here to dry my eyes ...
Being my strong and able man.

If there was separation (short),
It would not last very long,
And when we focus not on ourselves
We could see just what went wrong.

I want again to write those dreams
That seemed to disappear.
Did I kind of imagine them all?
Or were they actually here?

Was I supposed to follow through
Adjusting on their behalf?
Or was it written those dreams are gone
Well, that would make me sad?

I'm guessing I will never know
If my dreaming should now retire,
Or if for real I'll see those days
And achieve my heart's desire.

But I am compelled to remember
Some dreams of mine came true,
And whenever the Lord decides himself,
I'll get just what I'm due.

February 7, 2015

To the Graduates

Sometimes no one can see your plight.
Young people too can cry;
Oft times it's easier to shrink away
Than wait for aches to die.

When confronted with a justice call,
It's simple to claim your right,
But justice takes true courage
You can accept it or you fight.

In a state of calm and quiet
Your rage may be unseen
The fire has not yet burned out,
Or you crave what could have been.

Right now would be a perfect time
To reach out for your star;
If you can set your vision now,
It shouldn't be very far.

A message of hope to fulfill you,
Compressed in every step,
Achieve the once impossible
For one deserving—*yourself!*

For a test does not take always,
So let life be your song.
Enrich your lives with excellence,
And stay forever young.

September 26, 1990

To Stephen

I could recognize you, Stephen,
If I only heard you talk,
And maybe at a distance
I would recognize your walk.

If the day was nice and humid
And the sun was shining bright,
I could probably see your silhouette
And say, "That's Steve, all right."

But also what is certain
If I gazed a little while
I'd know that it was truly you
Because of how you smile.

You have an air about you,
And a pleasant side reveals
You treat everybody respectfully
No matter how you feel.

And that, I see, is a gift you have.
May I say it once again:
Always be encouraged
'Cause your neighbor is still your friend.

September 19, 2015

Togetherness

At night I look from my bedroom window;
I see the stars in the sky.
They shine when I look at them;
Sometimes I ponder why.

I think everything created
Has worth and beauty in it;
If you believe God covers you, too,
Then go ahead and say it!

The truth about the matter is
There's just not much concern
For things considered valuable,
Until we desire to learn.

Upon achieving some status,
We can develop a certain air,
"Don't walk with me as equal,
When you believe we can't compare."

It's so easy to be blinded,
But it does not have to be,
For if someone respects himself,
He should honor both you and me.

Giving's not always monetary,
Sharing a dollar or two,
It simply means you divide with me
And I will share with you.

It takes a world of grief sometimes
To show just how we stand;
Are we making every effort
To do all what we can?

There's nothing wrong with achievement,
It's hard to overcome,
Don't be shy to confess
The wrong things we have done.

It should not all be necessary;
It does not have to be.
Where can a generous soul exist?
Well, it's forever you and me.

July 10, 1971

Trying Harder

I used to try much harder
To keep myself in line,
But lately I've been tripping up;
I've gotten a bit behind.

Whenever I try to get where I
Just really plain don't care,
The consequence is struggles
I didn't have to bear.

So just this once I thought
I'd talk about it some;
At least this talk I'm doing now
I hope will do no harm.

Where is this now coming from?
What is my hurt and grief?
What's the complaining all about?
What sanity shall I keep?

To be perfectly honest,
I don't know for sure myself;
I am trying harder to understand
Many menacing things I've felt.

And just to think so many times
My intentions were nice and sweet;
I had a smile upon my face
For strangers I would meet.

I thought I was really okay,
Not too awfully bad;
Eventually I'd make up for
A few silly faults I had.

But looks like now it's different;

Somehow, there's been a change.
When I do some things I do,
It comes off very strange.

It seems a little bit harder
To get things really right;
I don't try to darken days
That others make so bright.

I wish I could revert to see
A simple, innocent me,
To keep guard on my tempers all,
Restrained and secretly.

What makes me question myself
Is I know it's wrong to start,
But I manage to still do it
Did I check my heart?

I can't forget some previous times
And actions in my past,
But I'm confident I am settled down,
For stress wasn't meant to last.

I must try to do at least
Today some kind of good;
I must achieve good things in life.
Learning, finally, how I should.

I'm on my way now hurriedly
I can briefly stop for rest,
But I want to not prolong the time,
And make some great progress.

January 28 and 29, 1971

Turning around Myself

Why am I troubled now this way?
I was just troubled the other day.
      And the day before that
      (Should I cry or laugh).
What clever words must I say?

Do I *not* know me very well?
Am I so like an infidel?
      I'm not used to being called worse;
      It makes me feel these newfound hurts.
Who in this world could ever tell?

Oh, let this sour taste depart!
Why take all tragedies to my heart?
      If I were flakes to fly away,
      It would not matter what others say.
I'd know to make a brave new start.

Many imitations around me be,
Faking it well, oh yes, I see.
      Should I hang my head in sorrow
      And decide to dread tomorrow?
Who's brave enough to answer me?

I am a woman—from a girl.
Let me try and change my world
      Or erase the ugliness that is left.
      Maybe just try to change myself,
      And then develop into a lovely pearl.

God willing, this soul is not done yet.
I know because the sun hasn't set;
      It was a day I still was touched,
      I don't think I missed too much,
I'll discard the bad, and keep all the rest.

April 25, 1984

Unwind

I know I've said a lot of things
And sometimes got off track,
Not certain of what I wanted
Or desired or especially liked.

Oh, I could be the sweetest thing
That you could ever know.
My solace could wrap a tarnished smile
And magnify its glow.

I'd give to you a morning
That lingers through the eve
With tenderness and ecstasy
That refuse to disperse or leave.

So sorry I had to hurry time
When between both you and I,
Or dampened that unplanned eagerness
That maneuvers us on high.

I gave you all the genuine *me,*
And it was right and real;
It's labeled loving heartbeats
And exposes the things I feel.

Some of me is soft and smooth,
Not really very tough,
I struggle sometimes with temperament,
But I control it well enough.

How amazing its capacity—
Simply marvelous, I would say;
I know because it's growing
Still larger day by day.

And with each sweet expansion,
Sincere words increase,
But I don't reveal the entire thing;
I'll choose to piece by piece.

And if I turn aside from you,
It is *not* my intent
To brush away your kindness
Like I do a speck of lint.

I just still seem to wrestle with
A shyness, not a void,
But I surely have not forgotten
The closeness we've enjoyed.

And so I say I do regret
I didn't take the time,
To comfort first and foremost
And help you to unwind.

September 10, 1991

Up the Praise

I realize you have prayed up
And acknowledge him every day;
I know you know, and so do I,
He's able in every way

To do whatever he wishes—
No problem with him at all.
He's even stationed angels
In case we slip or fall.

Humble but fervent praise goes up.
He is keeping us day and night.
May he bless our entire efforts
As we try to do what's right.

This moment I want to *up that praise*,
For his mercies are all brand-new,
Though I can't know what time is left
Or if my days be few.

But while I have the breath to breathe,
Please, Lord, just let me see
That I've done well in pleasing you.
This is my simple plea.

July 24, 2015

Use Your Gift

There are people more proficient
In sports or song or rhyme;
Intellectual types, when asked,
Have an answer every time.

Some folks have a special knack
Of dressing up just so.
They decide what they want to be
And where they want to go.

Early on, it's apparent
That their lives will be a thrill;
If at first they don't succeed,
Next time they probably will.

I bet you know a someone
Who is educated and wise;
They have it all together,
Or perhaps it's all a guise.

It can really get depressing
If you contend you're by yourself,
If all you've ever gotten
Was garbage that was left.

A messed up day, a muddled life—
Compressed onto a box.
You've wasted all your time, it seems,
Behind an exit that's locked.

I'm here now to say to you
You have another chance.
Make another brand-new start
And learn to laugh and dance.

There's not a certain trick
Or mystery where life's concerned;
It's whatever we've experienced
And what we all will learn.

You have a special gift, you know.
I think I have one too.
Let's tap into and use those gifts
So life won't be a zoo.

August 8, 1991

Valued Friend

I hope this finds you happy,
And you'll receive these
words just right.
A professional writer
might better say
Whatever thoughts I write.

I feel it is occasion—
That I write here to express
How difficult I think it is for you
To get things off your chest.

I did not tell you any lie
When I said that you're my friend,
And it means exactly
what it should
Until the unknown end.

Do I recognize you as valuable?
Can I see your greater task?
I wonder if you are angry,
And sometimes I want to ask.

It's conversation back and forth;
We both can have a voice.
Not *everything* is drama filled;
Sometimes our words get crossed.

To want a listening ear for you
And convince you in some way
I know just how to listen
To the boldness you do say.

I've experienced a few
brief moments
When you've allowed
me in your space
I've done the exact
same thing for you
As we shared a little grace.

One thing that seems
to resonate—
It bothers you, I know—
Is perhaps me making
a point of view
But getting there much too slow.

Well, maybe it's inherent.
It reminds me of the fact
That some of us have more to learn
With the load thrust on our back.

If perfection is what
we try to grasp,
Well, that will never be,
I'll resolve to protect
the friendship,
Being honest as I can be.

July 8, 2015

Wants

I want to thank you for being strong you,
Being patient in things I need you to.

I want to fight the blues I get
When sitting in front of TV set.

I want to cry when times get bad
Over all the moments we should have had.

I want to tell you my desire;
Baby, I want to fan your fire.

I want to come to you if ill;
I want to give you what you will.

I want to hear all things you say;
And understand in every way.

I want to grasp the misplaced thought
By forgiving them at the times I ought.

I want to just be close to you
In dark of night or morning dew.

I want to relish those kids of ours;
I want us all to smell the flowers.

If I must go before you do,
I want my heart to live with you.

April 21, 1987

Weak

How can I make *me* happy?
You're my one-in-a-million guy.
I'll just accept this abundance
Instead of questioning why.

Life is so unpredictable.
What power might I control?
Can others determine my fragile fate
If I do what I am told?

Acquaintances and friends aren't quite like me.
I go through things the most,
Living an ache inside my heart.
I will never get too close.

Whether or not they insult me
Or I bring things on myself,
I'll reach for the plate of plenty
And grasp what crumbs are left.

It's probably just another day,
And my feeling is at its peak;
I need compassion, sure and strong,
To help me where I'm weak.

July 30, 1992

Wedding Poem

Words of honor fill our hearts
As we think what Dad would say.
He'd say, "Go forth and celebrate
On this, your wedding day."

It's befitting on November 28
You made your vows and smiled.
His loving spirit escorted you
As you gracefully walked the aisle.

He watched over his baby girl,
And yes, some tears were wept,
He said he'd always love you;
That's a promise he made and kept.

He'd tell you don't be sad for him.
He's up in heaven—he'll see.
You deserve a perfect wedding day,
And he's as proud as he can be!

November 18, 2014

Welcome

Welcome to the house of God.
The spirit is here to share.
We invite you all to feel at ease.
We want to bow in prayer.

Oh Lord, we ask that through this hour,
We pray that souls are touched
We want to make them welcome
We worked and planned so much.

Dear God, forgive those sins we've done
And help us to belong,
To resist those things that tempt us,
We may not know are wrong.

Teach us truly Thy love for all
Until this life is through.
You've been so very merciful,
That's the least that we can do.

October 30, 1972

(Well, I Won't)

I've said, oh, plenty of times before
That I'm glad all dreams aren't true.
In fact I can't recall a time
It was pleasant all way through.

Some dreams were really awful
And very hard to take.
Then I'd be so *relieved*
When I would finally wake.

I'm starting to recognize at least
The choice I can control.
I surely don't have to live one day
When I quiver as if I'm cold.

I won't claim any more tragedy
From failures my life has seen.
I've repented and been delivered
And that was not a dream.

August 14, 2015

What Do I Expect?

How am I supposed to feel
When I'm starting to have these fears?
How can I clearly see my plight
When I'm looking through my tears?

Inside my head gets cold,
And inside my heart is warm.
Don't ask me any hard things now;
I want to do no harm.

Laughter is happy, or so I thought,
So shouldn't I feel a glow?
Mixing and mingling will help me, right?
With special ones I know.

I won't always bother them.
My urge is just to stay,
To quietly spend some time alone,
To sing a song and pray.

If you ask me now to tell you true
What I expect to do,
I'm hard pressed to just answer
For my words are usually few.

I don't think I have the luxury
To drag my feet and wait;
It would be mighty dangerous
To find *my* place too late.

I ask to get a timely peep.
I've not seen enough life yet,
But when I do it'll be all right,
And more than I expect.

August 15, 1991

What a Friend You Are

No matter how much I planned my life,
Not knowing where or when,
God saw a deepening loneliness,
So he sent to me a friend.

Just any strange person wouldn't suit me.
Friend waited afar somewhere,
Friend had to hurt a little bit, too,
But still show up to care.

Though *friend* might be a simple word,
Holy Spirit has let *me* see
Friend possess that love for Christ …
Which connects so much to me.

I thank you, God, for everything;
I have in you no fear.
The friend you sent to help me cope
Is abiding still strong right here.

You're awesome and you're wise, my Lord.
Please allow this special wish—
That an overflow of favor
Replenish what friend has missed.

I hope I've been a blessing, too,
You prepared me way back then,
So I just have to acknowledge *you*
And thank you for my friend!

March 3, 2015

What Would Jesus Do?

If you have gone a weary mile,
Depressed and scorned all the while,
And no one should be kind to smile
             ... what would Jesus do?

If through it all you find some light
To guide you to a greater height,
But something just won't work out right
             ... then what would Jesus do?

You don't know how to hold the tears
Because your "friends" have closed their ears,
But there's no reason to claim their fears
             ... so what would Jesus do?

Though by and by you will cross that stream,
Please don't give up on your dreams.
They're close at hand, or so it seems.
             ... See what Jesus can do?

You can do things half right yourself.
But be mindful of the gift he left.
You possess good life before your death
             ... so try doing what Jesus did.

December 28, 1972

Where Do I Go from Here?

I'm not feeling mad at life.
Frankly, I am just afraid;
It's like a flooded avenue
I'm compelled to personally wade.

I see it right in front of me,
And there's no one to help.
Borders are getting wider,
And I do not know its depth.

When my motions try to maneuver
To escape its raging stream,
There're obstacles all around me
That I have *never* seen.

I stubbed my foot on something hard;
My big toe has a bruise.
Do I not have one little thing
That I could maybe use?

So I contemplated what was next.
Then I backtracked to the trees.
That's where I saw a shaded spot
And felt more so at ease.

How can I safely get across
To bypass harm and risk?
Was there a detour sign back there
I possibly could have missed?

Stand still now and pray that God
Will tell me loud and clear
Where he wants my foot to tread?
Where do I go from here?

July 19, 2015

Who Loves You, Baby

I want to scream my cry so loud,
Then take it back somehow;
I am afraid to ask the truth.
Hey, do you hate me now?

Have I performed so casually
The phobia inside my head
That from the start did frighten me?
Have I done that thing I dread?

I've had the hardest possible time
Believing in myself,
And I refuse to totally trust
In especially someone else.

I don't expect perfection;
I'm not looking for all that's fair.
I want to know that *one* someone
Is in this world to care.

For if this was pre-destined,
And all was meant to be,
Then I only need to understand
The one who loves is me.

September 16, 1991

Wonderful Position (to Youths)

Imagine for the next few years
Someone would come to you
To tell exactly what's to come—
What things you ought to do.
They'd tell you very clearly
How to really achieve success,
To benefit from a good life,
And to avoid a lot of mess.
Managing to be a good person
Doesn't have to be a task;
Just do the thing that pleases God.
That's all, dear ones, he asks.
If you're not very confident,
Some things may seem absurd,
But check the scriptures for guidance;
Directions are in his Word.
So if you wonder how things will be,
What will your world look like?
Well, the Lord will guard and keep you,
And that's a given fact.
You're in a good position now—
No worry or doubt or fear.
Let God abide wherever you go,
Just like he's doing here!

November 5, 2015

Won't You Understand

You're tired. I'm tired. Oh, well.
Seems again we come to this.
Must misunderstanding each other
Be on our monthly list?

It's not only *you* and *me,*
But others display affect
Restless happening unplanned
Shouldn't be what all we get.

Have I just expected too much?
Each has his own desire.
The sun rose and set on both;
Perfection is just a liar.

I'd like to show me as I am.
And be ready to then confess,
I ask to have more patience,
Maybe then to avoid this mess.

My arms will only stretch to you,
And my soul is plenty wide;
Please don't drain my warmth that's left—
Don't leave me cold inside.

March 21, 1992

Wrap My Wound

I have a bunch of feelings
That are connected to this rhyme,
I almost said, "Don't do it,"
But I'm compelled to take my time.

It's kind of late ... and I should go.
The next day will draw near,
But I have need to write my heart,
Which ought not hold a fear.

I read about your promise, Lord,
So I'll stop asking why,
What pains besides this one,
Will I face before I die?

Tell me how to go about it
But not get ahead of you.
Prepare my ears to hear you
To know what things to do.

Put boldness in my belly
As you heal this hurting wound.
I know I'll understand it all
When I see you—oh, so soon.

September 20, 2015

You

Lord, I want to start this day
Excited to learn of you,
I want to not just look around
And miss all that is new.

For your written word has told me
I can ask whatever I will.
Father, I'm just asking please
To make me calm and still.

I'm feeling my way it seems
Through episodes not so nice.
Choices do come with consequence,
And I'm compelled to pay the price.

But there are times when looking back
I'm convinced it turned out right.
It was *you* who has enabled me,
Claiming victory in that fight.

So as the challenges loom this day
And I'm tempted to rave or pant,
Will I forget to praise *you*, Lord?
Oh no … I truly can't.

July 9, 2015

You Are

You are my gentle heart.
    If I rise up to feel its beat,
    I'm counting the times I wish I could say
        … I love you.

You are the other me
    Who came to me so young and free
    We got to know each other well, then I could tell
        … I love you.

You are my gift
    As a man, companion, and friend
    Who speaks when my soul breathes
    And the angels smile
        … I love you.

You are the unbroken link
    Connecting all that's wonderful in my life.
    How lucky I am to have you.
        … You are something to love.

January 5, 1994

You Sure?

I'm chatting quietly to myself today
(Counseling a little bit),
Trying to resolve a question—
I can't get away from it.

Why do I hear such nonsense
When I ask critics to convey?
It interrupts my solitude
On a simple, regular day.

Some wrong words definitely creep in
When I'm trying to state my views,
I work to try and tone it down
So I don't feel I'm used.

You can argue that I'm dreaming
Of things I sorely miss;
But their words are so compelling
I should put them on a list.

But don't you agree that if I want
To appear a bit more bold,
I cannot be so gullible
And believe everything I'm told.

Trying to acquire some wisdom,
Not all folks start out pure,
I don't want to jump too soon,
So I ask if I'm real sure?

July 27, 2015

Your Life

Considering how things existed,
I reckon change is due—
Maybe not to end the old
But to introduce the new.

Life is full of occasions
When over again we start
And realize we cannot avoid
An impromptu broken heart.

Life is for the living.
We get all we can get.
Fulfillments we remember,
But griefs we dare forget.

I try being optimistic
As I consider all my friends,
Hoping despair and discouragement
Will soon come to an end.

It's like you miss grandmother
With her gentle, insightful hand,
Something, someone, to grab hold
As only a grandma can.

Jump across those hurdles
With conviction as your mate;
In the meantime, look for happiness
No matter how long it takes.

February 4, 1992

Printed in the United States
By Bookmasters